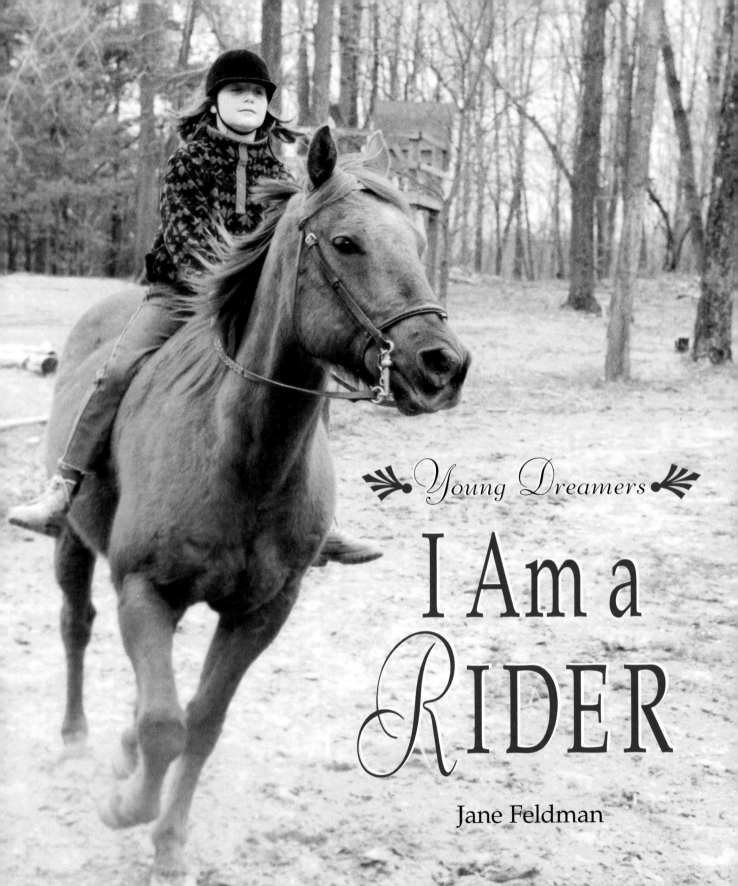

Young Dreamers

I Am a RIDER

Jane Feldman

Random House New York

To Lena, Kalina, Ayannah, Chamisa, Kelsey, Sarah, Tyson, Jannelle, Grayson, Phoebe, Ali, James Patrick, Michaelangelo, Emily, Alex, and McKenzie—the youngest dreamers of my extended family. They are my most constructive critics and surround me with constant inspiration. To all who love animals and to the animals who love us back. To knowing that we share a common planet. And to the dreamer in us all.

All rights reserved under International and Pan-American Copyright Conventions. Published in the United States by Random House, Inc., New York, and simultaneously in Canada by Random House of Canada Limited, Toronto. Distributed by Random House, Inc., New York.

www.randomhouse.com/kids

Library of Congress Cataloging-in-Publication Data
Feldman, Jane.
Young dreamers. I am a rider / by Jane Feldman. p. cm.
SUMMARY: Thirteen-year-old Eve Shinerock's mother is a riding instructor and Eve has her own horse, Lightning.
The story of the two of them growing up together is told in Eve's words and illustrated with Jane Feldman's photographs.
ISBN 0-679-88664-8 (trade) — ISBN 0-679-98664-2 (lib. bdg.)
1. Shinerock, Evening—Juvenile literature.   2. Shinerock, Evening—Pictorial works—Juvenile literature.
3. Show riders—Massachusetts—Biography—Juvenile literature.
I. Title: I am a rider. II. Title.
SF284.52.S45 F46 2000 798.2'3—dc21 99-056689

Printed in the United States of America April 2000 10 9 8 7 6 5 4 3 2 1

RANDOM HOUSE and colophon are registered trademarks of Random House, Inc.

There are many people (and horses) who have helped this dream come true. Many thanks to Eve, Amy, Robert, Laurel, and Solomon Shinerock for their graciousness and patience in allowing me to document a portion of their lives and for making it such a wonderful experience. And, of course, to Lightning for her gentle spirit.

To Kevin Wade, our wonderful blacksmith, and his daughter, Rachael, who will enjoy seeing Daddy at work in this book.

To Dr. Sue Tanner, whose long hours helping animals can now be recognized.

To Karen Carter for her help with our "horse show"…and especially to Amy Shinerock, whose work with horses and kids both educates and inspires.

To Karen Allen for introducing me to the Shinerock family.

To the Monadnock Waldorf School.

To Kate Klimo, Lisa Banim, Georgia Morrissey, Susan Lovelace, and Kenneth LaFreniere for their constant support and encouragement and for giving me the Young Dreamers series.

To Vicky Dwight (a horsewoman herself) and Chelsea Black & White Custom Lab for their encouragement.

To my Citykids and Darrow School families.

To my nuclear and extended family—with special thanks to my mother, whose unconditional love and support has been constant. To my dad (who gave me my first camera when I was thirteen) and Myra, my sister Jill and her family, and Birdie, my other mother.

To Erika Stone and Lari Brandstein (both have been mentors through the years), Melvin Estrella, Joanne Golden, Bill and Maria, and Michele McHugh; and to Helen Shabason for years of support.

And to the Creator—source of all creativity.

Hi! My name is Evening Shinerock, but everybody calls me Eve. This is my horse, Lightning. She's half Arabian and half Connemara pony.

I was only five when I got her. I'm thirteen now, so it seems like Lightning has always been part of my life. We make a great team!

This is my family. We live in western Massachusetts and we're all really close. As you can see, I'm the youngest. My sister Laurel is sixteen and my brother Solomon is seventeen. My mom and dad are both teachers. My mom teaches riding. I guess I'm pretty lucky!

I love looking at our family photo albums. Here's a picture of my grandma on horseback— in the middle of New York City!

Ever since we were little kids, my sister Laurel has always brought out my silly side.

We often look at the pictures together and remember things from years ago. Sometimes I show our albums to my friends, too.

This is one of the first times I ever rode Lightning. It was before I got her— I think I was three or four.

I've always spent a lot of time outdoors. Here I am in one of our flower gardens. Sunflowers are my favorite!

Mom and I took lots of long rides together. I rode Lightning and Mom rode our other horse, Happy.

When I was small, Mom used to give me a little boost up...but I was determined to do it myself!

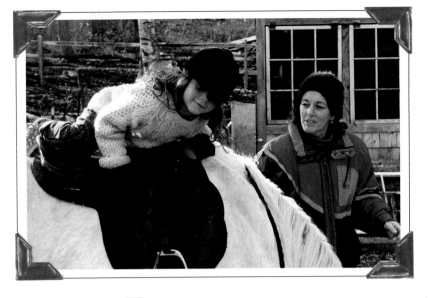

For Christmas one year, I made Lightning a special crown and brought her her favorite treat.

Laurel and I used to ride double on Happy.

When I was younger, Lightning and I used to enter competitions. It was exciting to see how well I'd learned all the things my mom had taught me. Sometimes I was a little nervous the morning of a big horse show, but when I got up on Lightning's back, she made me feel as if I could do anything.

The judges look for precision in both horse and rider. That means they have to work together well. A good rider keeps her heels down and her toes pointed in. She also keeps her hands absolutely still, with a gentle curve to her wrists and her thumbs pointed up. (Mom always had to remind me about that!) It's very important to keep your reins snug...but *never* to pull at the horse's mouth.

Lightning and I won lots of ribbons. I don't know who was prouder, me or her! My whole family and a bunch of my friends always came to our shows. It was great to know they were out there supporting us.

Some people think you control a horse just with the reins, but that's not true. There are four aids in riding: legs, weight, hands, and voice. To turn right, for instance, you gently move your weight to your right seat bone. When you want to stop, you brace your back and sink your weight deeper into your saddle. You should never kick a horse to make him go. That's like a punishment for the horse. Instead, you should ask your horse to move ahead by squeezing with your calves.

Even though Lightning and I don't compete much anymore, I still practice everything I learned. I especially love to jump.

You have to concentrate really hard so that you and your horse become almost one. I always listen to the rhythm of Lightning's strides and her breathing. Jumping is an amazing feeling!

Mom says my back could have been a little straighter going over this jump. Oops! Whenever I make a mistake, I go back and try again.

Lately, I'm more into trail riding than competing. It's a terrific way to really get to know your horse. I think it also teaches you respect for animals and nature. Another nice thing about trail riding is that you can go by yourself or with a friend. Sometimes my whole family goes out together.

There are many acres of trails on our land. Our next-door neighbors are "horse people," too, so they don't mind if we wander onto their property. Some trails are more challenging than others, with steeper hills or thicker woods.

Trail riding gives you a great sense of freedom. Another nice thing is that you can do it in all four seasons. That way, the trails always seem to look different.

Lightning has her favorite trails—and so do I! We take turns choosing.

After a long ride on a cold winter day, there's nothing better than heading home for a huge cup of hot cocoa!

Mom teaches English-style
riding as well as trail riding.
Sometimes she asks me to
help her get the horses ready
before her students arrive.
There's always a lot to do.

First we get the horses, and
then the saddles and bridles.
We also have to put together
the grooming kit.

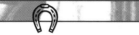

It's always a good idea for beginning riders to spend time grooming the horses at the start of a lesson. It gives them confidence around such big animals. It's also a sign of respect for the horses.

Today, we braided Lightning's tail. For shows, we often braid both her tail and her mane. You never leave the braids in too long, just like you wouldn't with *your* hair!

Because Lightning is such a gentle horse, she's had a lot of student riders. Her youngest was three—and her oldest was seventy-eight! Sometimes I get a little jealous sharing Lightning with other people, but I know that she's my special friend.

After grooming and getting to know the horses, it's time to saddle up. One of the first things Mom asks her students to do on horseback is to put their hands on top of their heads. That helps them find their "center." It's a very important part of riding.

We work mostly in the ring at first. Mom and I walk beside the students and their horses so the kids can feel more comfortable and get used to the strides of the horses. We also play games to develop balance. The kids touch their toes and reach to the sky. Sometimes Mom throws a softball to the riders, which they have to catch and throw back. It may sound a little crazy, but everyone has fun—and the games really help the kids learn to ride.

Some of Mom's students are serious competitors, but I work mostly with the trail-riding students.

Today, I helped two sisters ride on Lightning together, just like Laurel and I used to do. I think it made the little sister feel less nervous. The girls thought Lightning looked like a big teddy bear in her thick, woolly winter coat!

It's very important to cool the horses down before bringing them back to the barn. We teach the kids that caring for horses is a lot of responsibility: the constant shoveling and cleaning of stalls, feeding, and grooming and the regular cleaning and oiling of the saddles and bridles, which we call the tack. It's a *lot* of work—but I definitely think it's worth it.

On the way to the barn, Lightning saw that the hay truck was coming. That made her pretty excited! We have hay delivered once a month. An average horse eats half a bale of hay each day. Our horses also get grains in the morning and at night.

It takes a while to unload all of the hay. Usually, it takes one or two people, and they deliver fifty bales at a time. Our hay comes from a farm nearby.

Since the kids were still around during the hay delivery, Mom thought it would

be fun to finish class in the barn. It made the barn feel kind of like a clubhouse. ·

Kevin, the farrier, came today. A farrier is a blacksmith who works only with horses. Blacksmithing is a very old profession that is often passed down from generation to generation.

Kevin visits about every six weeks to make shoes for Happy. Lightning's hooves are very hard and strong, so she doesn't need shoes. Hooves are like fingernails—they grow constantly and have to be trimmed. The horseshoe has to be fiery hot before it can be put on a horse. It doesn't hurt the horse, though.

Our veterinarian is Dr. Sue Tanner. She gives Lightning a complete physical once or twice a year. She also gives her a shot to protect her from insect bites.

Dr. Tanner sees all kinds of animals. Her specialty is horses, but as she's a country vet, her patients vary from guinea pigs to mountain lions. Last week, she had a fawn in her office!

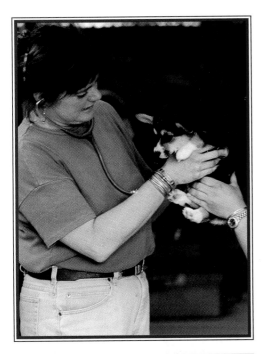

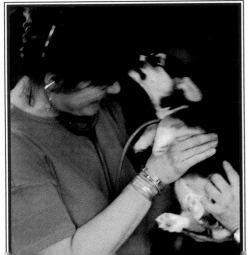

A neighbor brought a sick puppy over when she heard Dr. Tanner was here. Sometimes a vet runs the risk of being bitten or kicked when the animals are scared, but as you can see, the puppy had nothing but kisses for Dr. Tanner! Most animals can tell when you're trying to help them.

One of the best things about our house is that, no matter what room you're in, you can always look out and see the horses.

Each season is beautiful and brings its own special things.

In the winter, we get lots of snow. But waking up before sunrise on those freezing cold mornings to feed and check on the horses can be kind of tough!

Spring in the Berkshires brings new grass and flowers. It also brings the mud season, which is very difficult on the horses. The mud is deep and cold to walk through.

The summer is my favorite time of year—but probably not Lightning's. That's because the flies buzz around the horses and drive them crazy! Sometimes the flies get inside their ears.

Fall is pretty amazing in this part of the country. Tourists arrive from all over to see the foliage. Behind our house, we have mainly ash trees. When the leaves fall, they make a gold carpet on the ground.

This is the only home I've ever known. But life is about changes. Mom and Dad called a family meeting one night to let me, Laurel, and Solomon know that we'd be moving soon. My dad got a new job teaching in New Hampshire.

We kids weren't totally surprised. We knew Dad had been interviewing in several different places. But somehow, the possibility of moving hadn't seemed that real...until now. It was going to be hard to leave a place we all knew and loved so well.

We started to pack a million boxes and say good-bye to our friends. One of the hardest parts of moving, though, was knowing that things would never be quite the same for me and Lightning. Our new house in New Hampshire didn't have land set up for horses. That meant we'd have to find somewhere else nearby for them to live, at least for a while. Mom told me that we could visit the horses often. But I knew it wouldn't be the same as knowing they were right out back.

In between packing and helping with the move, I spent as much time with Lightning as I could.

The move itself went pretty smoothly. Dad drove up first with the horses to get them settled into their new home. Lightning and Happy each had special trailers.

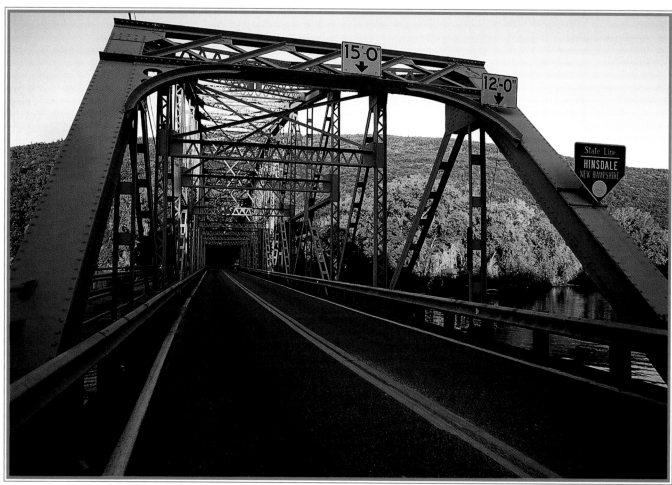

Mom, Laurel, Solomon, and I drove the moving truck up a week later. The drive from Massachusetts to New Hampshire took about four hours. You can't travel too fast in a big, clunky van!

When we finally got there, it was great to have the whole family reunited. Well, *almost* the whole family. The new house was really nice, but I knew I'd have some adjusting to do. Mom promised we'd visit Lightning and Happy just as soon as we were settled in.

EQUESTRIAN XING

One of the best things about our new house is—
MY ROOM! It's huge. In the old house, I had the
smallest bedroom because I was the youngest. I
put all my ribbons up on my dresser to remind me of Lightning and our horse shows.

Everyone knew how much I missed having Lightning around. So they got me a
kitten. I named her Zelia. It helped
to have a fuzzy friend around...even
though I still missed Lightning.

In the beginning, I really missed all
of my old friends back home, too. But
we called and wrote to each other
every week.

One afternoon, Mom and I went shopping for clothes. That made me feel a little better about starting a new school!

I went out exploring around our house. New Hampshire is a lot like the Berkshires, but the mountains are higher.

Starting a new school is always a little tough. But having to ride there with Dad an hour before the other kids arrived was definitely an adjustment. It was a whole new experience having Dad teach at *my* school!

I have to admit, moving was a big change, and sometimes I felt kind of sad, especially about Lightning. But in the end, I think it was good for all of us and I'm happy now.

This year I have a woodworking class. Guess what one of the first things I carved was?

Finally, it was time for me and Mom to visit Lightning and Happy. They both were being very well cared for by Karen, the woman who was boarding them. Lightning was so happy to see me. She nuzzled against me for a long time. I could tell she was happy in her new home, though. There were other horses there and they all seemed to get along well.

After I took Lightning out to the barn, I went back for Happy. She couldn't wait for me to get her, too. She gets sort of hyper sometimes if she feels she's being left behind. Mom says I have a calming effect on the horses.

After we groomed Lightning and Happy, Mom and I took them for a long ride.

Mom has plans to resume her riding lessons here—and, of course, I plan to help! There are lots of new kids interested in riding both Lightning and Happy.

Mom and Karen thought it would be fun to introduce us to some of the students by having a rather informal "horse show." Some kids came to ride, and others just to watch.

I got a chance to ride Lightning and I realized I still remembered almost everything from when I used to compete. It felt great!

I mainly helped the younger kids. There were several different competitions. The one the kids seemed to like best was where they had to go around the ring holding a full glass of grape juice. Whoever spills the least wins!

Lightning likes to drink whatever's left when the riders are done.

Since it wasn't a traditional horse show, at the end of the day we decided to give *everyone* a ribbon! That made all the kids proud. Competing is fun, but it's not everything. It's just as important to believe in yourself and feel confident.

We hope to have Lightning come to live with us again someday soon. But no matter where I live or what I do in the future, I know that Lightning and I will always be together in spirit...and I will always be a rider!

Jane Feldman is a professional photographer whose striking work has gained international attention in the field of advertising and among nonprofit organizations that promote youth empowerment. This is Ms. Feldman's second book. She is currently working on her next project in the Young Dreamers series, *I Am a Gymnast*. A native New Yorker, Ms. Feldman divides her time between Manhattan and the Berkshire Mountains in Massachusetts.